Humility To Greatness

A Story of Resilience in the Face of Adversity

Kelley Ann Smith

Copyright © *Kelley Ann Smith*, 2025

All Rights Reserved

This book is subject to the condition that no part of this book is to be reproduced, transmitted in any form or means; electronic or mechanical, stored in a retrieval system, photocopied, recorded, scanned, or otherwise. Any of these actions require the proper written permission of the author.

Table of Contents

Dedication 1

Forward 3

Introduction 4

Early Stages 6

Mr. Charlie 13

Hard Work 20

Grandma 26

The Big Move 31

GM 38

Largest Family in the Block 44

To Future Generations 52

Words To Live By 58

About the Author 64

References 65

Dedication

To my beautiful children: Aliyah, Amirah, Olivia, and James:

The four of you have shown me what true unconditional love looks and feels like. Throughout our lives together and the many challenges we've had to face, you depict a level of resilience that rivals even the strongest of people. My prayer is that this book will show you where your strength comes from and that you can conquer the world. May every day of your life be a testament to all you have endured and a shining light toward all you will accomplish.

"I can do all things through Christ who strengthens me."
Phillipians 4:13

To my Kimmy:

"To be great is to be misunderstood." – Ralph Waldo Emerson

Leading by serving others.
Maintaining in the midst of chaos.
Loving in a world of hate.
Praying when no one is watching.
These describe the very essence of who you are, a child of God with a bright light illuminating every space you walk in. May the Lord forever keep your light shining for a brighter tomorrow.

"Let your light so shine before men, that they may see your good works, and glorify your Father which is in heaven."
Matthew 5:16

Forward

My youngest daughter, Olivia, was in the 7th Grade. She came home from school one day a little discouraged. "Mom, every single book we are assigned to read is just sad," she said. She was right. These books were about the loss of a parent, children wandering in the wilderness, children in war-torn countries, and other tragedies. I don't think this was intentional. I believe that teachers choose these books because they align with the various literary lessons in the school curriculum.

The problem is, we live in a world with tragedy all around us. Wars and conflicts affect every nation on the planet in some capacity. Acts of violence plague every community in the United States. It's not only urban but rural communities as well. Newscasts, articles, and social media posts report injustice locally and abroad. The pitfalls of life affect the rich and the less fortunate. From school shootings and racial tension to political strife and mental health struggles, no one is exempt.

I wrote this book to provide another option and to share pieces of my grandfather's life that many may not know. I hope to provide a fresh perspective for all, no matter what stage of life you are in. Life can throw some unexpected curveballs at you. It's how you catch them that matters!

Introduction

There he stood in the middle of the street. He was smiling from ear to ear. His cheeks were big and round. His eyes were squinted from his high cheekbones and the rays of the sun, almost like a Siamese cat. He stood about 5 feet 5 inches tall. His hands were on his hips, proudly admiring as if he had built the house all by himself.

The weather was rather warm for a fall day in North Carolina. The temperature that morning was 74 degrees at 9:30 am, hinting at another day in October that would prove to be a record breaker. The sky appeared to be a vibrant azure blue with not a cloud in sight. The sun illuminated every aspect of the scene, adding a personal touch to every tree and blade of green grass. An occasional burst of wind would blow, bringing just enough cool air to forewarn that a shift in the atmosphere was on the way.

Meanwhile, I brought my grandmother, mother, and father inside for a tour. We entered my living room slowly with the anticipation of a warm and cozy atmosphere. Hints of burgundy flowed throughout the room, adding an elegant pop of color and grandiose feel. The next room was the kitchen, with its bright yellow walls that seemed to sparkle from the sunlight. With floral pictures on the walls and red vases that graced the top of the cabinets, the kitchen gave the idea of a farmhouse out in the country. Walking through to the dining room gave an aura that only the family can understand.

Wondering where my grandfather was, I walked outside to find him walking around in the backyard. The bumblebees and dragonflies circled his head as if welcoming him to their world. The brown speckled house finch, which had a nest in a nearby tree, flew over to inspect the new visitor. A level of curiosity crept over me, so I decided to join him. He was bent over studying the foundation of the house, every crack and crevice.

But...wait...let us go back to where it all began.

Early Stages

The air was crisp with a breeze alternating between warm and cold. The leaves danced erratically on the trees as if they knew today was their last. The sun shone even brighter than ever, ushering in a new season filled with endless possibilities. It was the 21st day of October in McColl, South Carolina. A new generation was born. One that would no doubt affect the trajectory of future generations to come.

She looked down upon him proudly, as if she were gazing into the universe. His puffy cheeks stood out the most on his small, round face. His eyes were squeezed tightly together. His hands were clenched in the shape of a fist. He waved them about as if he were already mad at the world and ready for the fight of his life. He was swaddled in a small cotton blanket of gray and white stripes. After his initial cry, the soft cooing of a newborn baby could be heard throughout the tiny shack in the middle of the cotton field. The infant was my grandfather.

The tiny home was typical of the era for poor black people. It sat alone in the middle of a field. Cotton grew wild, so it was everywhere and could be seen for mile-long stretches at a time. It was in fields all over the south. The shack was made of wooden planks that were worn and chipped. The floor creaked with even the slightest movement. The roof was a metal tin hanging lopsided over the wood planks. The walls were lined with newspapers to block out the chill. There was just one room, barely enough for a family to live in. An old black iron stove sat in the middle, used to heat the space and cook meals. A small tin tub was tucked into a corner, with a curtain hung for privacy. All water for bathing and cooking came from the well. There was a small outhouse about 100 feet from the shack. An outhouse was a small building separate from the house. It had a toilet without plumbing that sat over a pit. For fear of snakes and other animals, a slop jar would be used during the night and emptied every morning. A slop jar was an old jar used in place of a toilet overnight. Everyone with an outhouse had one, and one of the family members was responsible for emptying it every morning. All in all, the shack provided shelter from the elements and a place to call home.

His family life was much like many others in the South. Susie, his mother, raised five daughters and two sons on her own. As a Black woman, she relied on a mix of trades to make ends meet. Cooking, cleaning, and sewing were the most common skills passed down through the generations. Because of the region, cotton was the main crop and grew wild everywhere. She mainly picked cotton to support her family. Any one of these occupations would provide just enough income to survive another day. "One day at a time, sweet Jesus. That's all I'm asking of you," she would sing. Notes of soprano heard with an underlying hint of heaviness that only her life could bring. Somehow, music provided an escape from life as she knew it. Her childhood seemed a distant memory, a past she could hardly remember. Her present and future were filled with anxious hope only a mother would know.

*

Life during the 1930s was tough. The stock market crash of 1929 sparked the worst economic crisis in U.S. history.

Banks and other financial institutions soon failed. People across the country felt hopeless. No matter their background, everyone was affected. Despair was seen with the rich as well as the poor. To survive, black people would hide their money in mattresses, wall outlets, and even slop jars. These were clean, new slop jars, of course, but a thief would never think to look there. Susie would hide her money so well, she often forgot where she put it. Albert was good at finding things and great at finding money. So, she would call on him for a second pair of eyes, and he would find the cash in no time at all. Even though he was young, they worked together as a team, making sure the family had everything they needed.

The Great Depression made it very challenging to buy food. Mama Susie would grow what she could in a small patch of land behind the shack. Tomatoes, cucumbers, mustard greens, and green peppers were always easy to grow. A few pinto and green bean vines grew alongside the small garden. On the left side of the tiny home, a few squash and zucchini plants would yield enough to help sustain them through summer and fall. There were always chickens running around, too. They had fresh eggs whenever they were available. Chicken was eaten once a week. Susie would ring the neck, remove the feathers, and cook the chicken in a pot. Other than these foods, Susie would rarely be able to purchase sugar, flour, and other necessities. However, she was very creative in the kitchen. She would see 5 ingredients and make a full meal. One of her specialties was a summer stew made from tomatoes, onions, squash, zucchini, and carrots. Beans were always the cheapest food to purchase so that she would make a pot of pinto beans and butter beans regularly. With a pinch of salt and pepper, these beans would taste and smell so good. Somehow, God always provided enough food to sustain them.

Jim Crow laws was yet another issue Albert had to contend with. Nearly everything was separated by Whites Only and Colored Only signs. The entrances to the banks, government buildings, stores, and shops were all labeled accordingly. Front entrances had White Only signs, and back entrances had Colored Only signs. Some of the restaurants had separate entrances. Black people had to go around the back of these restaurants to be served. Others didn't serve black people at all and had Whites Only signs on the front door. The bathrooms and water fountains inside all the buildings were also separated. This was the only way of life Albert knew while growing up.

Schools were separated, with different buildings for Black and white students. Albert walked through open fields to reach the dirt road that led to his school. The "Colored Only" building had crumbling concrete steps. The roof was in desperate need of repair because rays of sunshine would come through distracting the students from learning. The dark wood flooring squeaked with every step. The cream-colored walls had peeled so badly that they exposed the wood planks behind them. The desks and chairs were used, handed down from the White Only schools when they had no more use for them. The desks had old pencil marks, and the chairs were peeling on the legs, but still sturdy. The teacher had a used desk and chair, also, usually made of heavy oak. The books and writing materials were used as well, but served the purpose of learning. The teachers did their best to use everything wisely. Though the school building was worn down, the kids showed up ready to learn, believing it would help them give their families a better life when they grew up.

The students were taught the basics. Math focused on addition, subtraction, multiplication, and division. All the teachers knew that a strong foundation in Math would carry the students a long way in life. Much of the school day was spent on reading though. Comprehension was very important because many Black people at the time were illiterate. They worked in the fields and made money working in other people's homes. Many did odd jobs and had side hustles or side jobs to supplement. However, a generation with strong reading skills would have better opportunities and access to better-paying jobs. History was taught with a mixture of American and World Studies. Most of these lessons came from the old, donated textbooks they were using. Aware of the times they were living in, the teacher would often add current events to help the students relate. Included in the curriculum would be Black History lessons so the students would know where they came from and what their ancestors had been through. Some basic Science lessons were taught from the old textbooks also. Students learned about nature, astronomy, the body, and earth sciences. Other than the textbooks, teachers passed down their own wisdom and knowledge gathered during their life experiences.

Many days, Albert found himself dreaming about being outdoors instead of sitting in a classroom. The open fields and fresh air gave him a sense of freedom from the struggles at home. Every morning while walking to school, he would gaze at the various birds flying around. Blue Jays, Robins, black Crows, Mourning Doves, and Carolina Chickadees were just a few of the birds he saw regularly. Occasionally, a Red-Tailed Hawk would circle high in the sky, looking to swoop down for lunch. "They always seemed so busy," he thought. The wildflowers along the dirt road conveyed a message that something beautiful can grow from something as plain and dull as dirt. They were every color in the spectrum, from bright white to indigo blue. The fields of cotton seemed to go on forever. They served as a constant reminder that there is always work to do. His mother would tell him and his siblings about her parents' struggles with manual labor and how grateful her children should now be. She always saw the brighter side of life and encouraged them that better days are coming. Albert felt deep down inside that she just might be right.

After school, Albert had duties no child his age had ever seen. As the oldest son, he was automatically considered the "man of the house." Every obligation and responsibility this title held applied to him. His duties included fetching water from the well, going to the market with his mother, gathering the vegetables from the garden, and tending to the chickens. He also fixed things as needed around the tiny shack, such as patching up holes in the walls. Gathering wood for the black iron stove was the hardest and most strenuous chore of all. He had to go into the nearby woods and chop some small trees down for their wood. It got easier as he grew older, though. Taking care of his younger siblings was expected. He helped his little brother learn how to tie his shoes and button his shirt. He taught him a few chores so he'd be prepared to pitch in later on. He also showed his sisters how to draw water from the well for daily use. His role as an older brother gave him a sense of pride.

Albert's early stages of life were filled with adult responsibilities. It was a difficult balance between acting his age and growing up. But he was born with the ability to withstand even the hardest of situations and overcome any obstacle in his path. The expectation to provide for and help protect the family of 8 served as a precursor to the rest of his life.

Mr. Charlie

At just 12 years old, Albert turned the key and started the tractor. He felt like the weight of the world rested on his shoulders. With the family in need of money, he left school in the 7th grade and began working for Mr. Charlie. Back then, this kind of responsibility wasn't unusual. Children would have to help support the family in any way they could. The daughters would help by cleaning houses or doing alterations on clothing. The sons would do more of the manual labor jobs, such as driving tractors, farming, and other odd jobs. All these jobs paid a wage that the children brought back to their families. It taught them life skills that they would use for the rest of their life.

He plowed the fields daily after harvest time and earned a wage enough to feed the family. Mr. Charlie worked with him all day long, teaching him how to plow the fields. He taught Albert how to steer and stop the tractor. He showed him how to plow in straight lines, so all the land was covered. It took Albert some time because the big brown tractor was old and would stop running occasionally. He paid close attention to everything Mr. Charlie said. He also asked lots of questions to gain a better understanding. He worked day and night trying to perfect this new skill. The fields were no match for him once he got the hang of it, though.

*

Mr. Charlie was a nice white man, honest and fair to everyone. He was born and raised in South Carolina. His parents were sharecroppers at first, working the land day and night. They saved enough money to buy 30 acres of land and start their own farm. They taught him everything he knew about farming. He inherited all the land, including their farm, when they died. This land had been with the family for as long as he could remember. His land extended far across McColl, South Carolina. Cotton was a major crop in the South. Acres and acres of land were devoted specifically to this crop. White cotton plants blanketed the fields as if soft, fluffy clouds had fallen from the sky. My ancestors from long ago were forced to work endlessly in these same fields for free. Now, Albert and others like him worked for a wage.

On his land, Mr. Charlie had a farm with lots of animals. On any given day, Albert could see as many as 100 chickens running around several chicken coops outside of the big red barn. The lone rooster would strut with his head held high, ready to start the day. Beside the chickens was a rather large pig pen with a feeding trough nearly 25 feet long. Pigs and hogs of all sizes wallowed in the mud, creating such a mess that they all appeared the same brownish-gray color. Several gray and white goats wandered around outside of the pig pen. They ate grass and weeds, and were the easiest to maintain, feed, and care for. They stayed close by and were also the easiest to manage. Mostly, they were good for keeping the land trimmed, often seen wandering across the fields. That might explain why Mr. Charlie's property always looked freshly cut.

A little way down, just passed the red barn, was an open field of grass. This is where the cattle grazed. Mr. Charlie had 14 cows and 4 steers. The cows produced enough milk for his family and the community. His wife and children would help him bottle the milk and sell it in town. They would always give Albert a bottle for free. When a cow was too old to produce milk, it would be slaughtered. Susie loved slaughtering time because she would always get some fresh beef. Those were some of the best dinners ever.

People passing through would admire his property and how beautiful it was. Several local artists asked if they could come to paint pictures of the main house. It was a stately house, white with black shutters. It stood 2 stories tall with an outside porch off the first and second floors. It had large, grand windows that reflected the sun's light. The laurel bushes close to the house were neatly trimmed and roundly shaped. They appeared almost to hug the house naturally. The willow and oak trees surrounding the house were so tall and had thick clumps of moss hanging off their branches. The best portraits were painted after a light rain, when the entire scene seemed to sparkle.

Other paintings of the property were of the barn area. The large red barn sat amid all the farm animals. It was 2 stories high with 4 open windows on each side. It had double doors in the front and in the rear. These paintings captured the chickens and pigs walking around them. They showed the goats in the surrounding fields eating grass. Off in the distance was the cow pasture with the cows standing and sitting close together in groups. They were black, brown, and spotted. One of them was white. Mr. Charlie had the only white cow in town. Some painters would come just to paint a picture of it. Above the living room fireplace hung a portrait of Mr. Charlie's house, and in the kitchen was a picture of his barn.

Though he lived there every day, he never got tired of admiring his home.

Also, Mr. Charlie had an array of crops. His farmland held every type of vegetable one could name. He grew plenty of root vegetables like carrots, turnips, celery, onions, potatoes, and radishes. There were rows and rows of leafy greens such as lettuce, mustard greens, spinach, collard greens, and cabbage. He had half an acre of corn with stalks as high as 6 feet tall. He always allowed Albert to pick some of the ears of corn and bring them home. The tomatoes and cucumbers grew in abundance all over. But Albert always wondered why his mother's tomatoes were larger, healthier, and riper. Susie said plants are alive and if you sing and talk to them, they grow bigger and stronger than ever. Susie sang to her plants every morning, thankful for all they produced.

The grove of fruit trees seemed to stretch far across the property. There were 6 tall apple trees with red apples everywhere. These apples had the sweetest taste. There were 8 plum trees with small, round, juicy purple fruits. These trees carried a low hum and soft soothing sound from all the honeybees and bumblebees that circled around them. The pear trees at the end seemed to struggle at first, but produced a fair amount of fruit late in the summer. It was hard to tell if they were ripe because the outside skin was so firm. Mr. Charlie always knew, though. At the end of the row were a few young pear trees reaching daily for the sun.

Just beyond the fruit trees was a small plot of land full of dark green watermelon plants. Mr. Charlie had the sweetest watermelons in town. They ranged in size from medium to large, oval-shaped, and had dark green stripes. He always gave Albert the largest one to take back home. The cantaloupes grew on a vine so long that it seemed to go on forever. Albert knew when they were ripe because he could smell their aroma from several feet away. Next to the cantaloupes grew honeydew melons. It was hard to tell if they were ready to pick, but Mr. Charlie was an expert. The bright, light green color inside each melon showed Albert that even though the melons appeared dull on the outside, the inside was perfectly ripe.

*

Albert picked up a lot from Mr. Charlie. He showed him how to till and clear the land in winter, when to plant seeds in early spring, and how to care for young plants. Mr. Charlie also taught him how to prune the crops so they'd grow strong, healthy vegetables. Albert was constantly pulling off dead leaves and cutting unproductive limbs off the fruit trees so the nutrients would go directly to the fruit. This made the fruit plump and ripe faster than any others. During harvest time, Albert would join the rest of the farm workers in helping to gather all the fruits and vegetables. This would occur throughout the summer and fall and was a massive group effort. After everything was sorted and organized, Mr. Charlie would sell his harvest of food at the local market. Albert loved to help, especially since Mr. Charlie would give him a basket to take home.

During that era in time, everyone shared what they had. If someone needed some sugar, they simply asked a neighbor. If someone else needed a few eggs, they would ask a neighbor.

Other than selling in the market, Mr. Charlie would lend a helping hand to anyone in need. Even the low-income families with children would get some of the fruits and vegetables that Mr. Charlie would set aside specifically for them. He always said to remember the less fortunate because we all need a little help at some point in our lives.

Albert considered Mr. Charlie a father figure. His own father left him and his family years ago. Feelings of low self-esteem plagued him as a child due to his fatherless home. He would sometimes question his ability to complete certain tasks, such as plowing the fields in straight lines and remembering all his responsibilities at home. The pressure to try and fill this adult role caused a level of anxiety not experienced by anyone around him. Mr. Charlie saw the nervous yet optimistic glimmer in Albert's eyes and knew he needed encouragement. He motivated Albert to push forward while guiding him through every task on his work list. One such task was pruning the fruit trees. If the trees were not pruned properly, they wouldn't yield much fruit and could accumulate diseases. Mr. Charlie taught Albert how to trim each fruit tree and check for signs of disease. He often praised Albert for working hard and paying close attention. That encouragement gave Albert the boost he needed to feel proud of himself. As time went on, his confidence greatly increased.

Mr. Charlie was an excellent role model and example for the community. Every day of his life, he portrayed a love for all living things. His animals on the farm were some of the best, well-kept livestock in the southeast. They were treated almost as if they were family. The workers on the farm followed his example and cared for the animals with great consideration. And as for the workers, Mr. Charlie paid them a fair enough wage so that they could provide for the needs of their families. He treated all of them with respect and compassion. Some of them looked forward to working on Mr. Charlie's farm. Albert took notice of this and vowed never to forget it because it was so rare to see a farm run with love.

Working on the farm paralleled the various seasons of life itself. Tending to the crops and working in the fields reminded him that there is a time to plant and a time to harvest. Throughout his life, Albert would learn that there would be times when he had to make sacrifices in the beginning, just to reap the benefits in the end. For example, dropping out of school at such a young age to work was a huge sacrifice, but the knowledge he obtained while working on the farm proved very valuable in adulthood. The temperature during the summer was always hot in South Carolina. However, sometimes it would be extremely hot for weeks at a time. Crops such as beans, squash, and corn would suffer and would not produce as much. Albert observed this decrease in crops and thought about something his mother would often say. Life is full of highs and lows. Some seasons were rich with harvest. Summer's watermelons, full and sweet, showed signs of a good year. Other seasons brought struggle. Dying crops showed just how hard life on the farm could be. These lessons followed Albert for the rest of his life and helped to shape the very essence of a family filled with love and resilience.

Hard Work

As Albert grew older, his expertise with manual labor grew. By age 14, he was proficient in farming. The foundation he gained while working with Mr. Charlie helped Albert develop the strongest work ethic in town. It was so strong that word about him spread for miles. Everyone was so impressed with a young man his age and his eagerness to learn. Soon, everyone was calling Mr. Charlie to try and reach Albert. His uncanny sense of responsibility and maturity level were well sought after, and someone like him was considered very valuable.

The first person to inquire about Albert was Mr. Wilson. He owned a local plumbing company and needed an apprentice. He went to visit Mr. Charlie's farm for some freshly laid eggs. While there, he saw Albert on the tractor in the middle of the field, his body barely visible over the large black steering wheel. Mr. Wilson motioned for Albert to come sit down and talk awhile. He explained everything there is to know about plumbing, such as how to install pipes and clear drains. Albert was eager to learn and later that week joined Mr. Wilson at his shop to start training. He was first taught how to identify all the different tools that plumbers use. Tools such as soft jaw pliers, wrenches, wire pipe cleaners, tube benders, and screwdrivers. Then he was taught to recognize all the different pipes and what they are used for. Soon, Albert was completing jobs on his own with all the knowledge of a great plumber.

Next, Mr. Rainey had a plumbing issue at his home. His sink drain was clogged, and no matter what he tried to do, nothing worked. Albert was sent to Mr. Rainey's house to unclog the drain. While there, Mr. Rainey noticed Albert's hard work and attention to detail in finding the problem and getting the job done. He decided to ask Albert if he had any interest in electrical wiring. Albert loved a challenge. Mr. Rainey owned an electric company in town that serviced the entire community. However, he needed some help. So later that week, Albert went to Mr. Rainey's shop to learn all about electrical work. He was introduced to a variety of tools such as insulated screwdrivers, electrical wire pliers, hole saw kits, wire strippers, and conduit benders. These tools were commonly used for fixing circuit breakers, faulty switches, loose outlets, and frayed wiring. He gained great knowledge as an electrician in a matter of weeks.

Finally, Albert was sent to Mr. Jones's house to check some wiring issues in his living room. The power seemed to flicker whenever someone walked around in the room. Albert put on his tool belt and started investigating. He soon discovered that the problem was some exposed wiring that could potentially cause an electrical fire. In the meantime, Mr. Jones noticed how serious Albert was with his work. He was impressed by the dedication and determination in Albert's eyes. The construction company on the outskirts of town was owned by none other than Mr. Jones. When all the electrical work was done, Mr. Jones asked Albert if he had an interest in construction. As always, Albert was more than eager to learn and accepted the offer. This undertaking exposed him to a whole new occupation. He learned how to use a nail gun, hand drill, masonry trowel, and sledgehammer. These tools were frequently used on tasks such as framing a structure, hanging drywall, installing flooring, and installing insulation. During the next month, Albert would go on to learn everything it takes to build and repair a home.

*

Back at home, Susie began to see her surroundings improve. Albert was making a decent amount of money from all his specialties. His mother and siblings had more and more of their needs met. He asked his new employers if he could have any leftover materials no longer needed. They obliged, and he began bringing those materials back home at the end of his workday. Starting with the house, Albert added 2 rooms with the leftover lumber from Mr. Jones's construction jobs. He patched up the sides of the roof that leaked during a heavy rain. He removed the newspaper from the walls and insulated each room with thick pink insulation material. He ripped all the old floorboards up and installed new flooring. The new flooring was solid oak planks that were thick and strong. He sealed the windows with caulk and applied fresh gray paint to the walls. The tiny shack now looked and felt like a small home, warm and cozy.

The family had more food than before. Each week, Albert got a basket of fresh fruits and vegetables from Mr. Charlie. But things like sugar, flour, and butter still had to be bought. Susie used their extra income to buy these and other items, and she was able to make fresh bread every few days. Also, meat of any kind was a hot commodity. The family only ate chicken on Sunday afternoons and occasionally beef when a cow was slaughtered, but this soon changed. They were able to afford pork chops and slabs of pork for bacon. She even had more beef for hearty stews that would feed the family for several days. The stew had chunks of tender beef along with carrots, peppers, cabbage, onions, and corn. A generous amount of fresh oregano and parsley was added for flavor topped with a dash of salt and black pepper to taste. Slow-cooked all day long on the old black wood-burning stove, the stew filled the home with a thick aroma of savory, bold flavors and the feeling of home. Family members living nearby would even visit just to get a bowl.

Clothing had been a bit of a challenge for the family of 8. The girls shared everything, such as dresses, skirts, shirts, socks, and even shoes, when possible. Susie would hem the dresses or let the hem out according to which daughter was wearing it. She was constantly adjusting for their alternating heights. Albert's younger brother had to wear all his hand-me-downs. Most of his shirts hung to his knees. He had to roll up the bottom of his pants so Susie could sew a cuff in them. His shoes would even flop because they were too big, and he hadn't grown much. This was the way of life for many of the families in the South.

Albert's new occupations drastically improved how they dressed. Susie was able to buy more fabric to make dresses for all the girls. She was able to buy extra fabric for shirts and pants for the boys. She purchased a pair of new shoes for the whole family. No more holes on the bottom or toes peeking out from the top. She even had enough fabric and thread to make a couple of new dresses for herself.

The family finally began moving towards a more stable condition. The house began to take on a rustic charm that the family could appreciate. It was noticeably cooler in the summertime and warmer in the winter. There was more space in the home, which made it easier for everyone to relax. The children started looking healthier and had more energy thanks to the regular, balanced meals. These meals helped give them the strength they needed. Their attire looked as if they were prestigious. Susie made bright yellow, green, and blue dresses with frilly lace on the hems. All the new shirts for the boys fit them perfectly.

The community also noticed. The children wore their new clothes to school. All their classmates were excited to see what they wore every day. The other children loved the bright colors and patterns so much that they asked if Susie could make clothes for them, too. Even the teachers were impressed and complimented them. In town, Susie would go to the local general store for necessary items such as sugar and flour. Everyone she passed on the street would compliment her dresses and shoes.

"Nothing ever comes to one that is worth having, except as a result of hard work." This quote by Booker T. Washington is one Albert stood on all his life. His spirit of determination and hope for a better tomorrow propelled him at an early age toward creating the life he only dreamed of having. His dreams of better living conditions were playing out right before his very eyes. A better, more livable home, plentiful food, and upgraded clothing fit for royalty were all he wanted. All of this was made possible by Albert, a steadfast young man who worked hard towards a better life for himself and his family.

Grandma

She had a touch of southern charm that no other woman for miles could rival. Her beautifully pressed curls looked like loose ringlets. Her sparkling dark-brown eyes were small, and when she smiled, barely seen. Her nose spread slightly across her face. She had full lips that, when parted, revealed a small gap between her 2 front teeth. Shiny metal earrings dangled from her ears like dewdrops. She stood 5 feet 5 inches tall. Her figure was very shapely, rather shapely for an 18-year-old. She walked with her head held high, confident with every move she made. Her glow would illuminate every room she entered. She was my grandmother.

She had several gifts, but her love for sports stood out. Running was her favorite; she would take off as fast as lightning and always outran the other girls. She spent hours playing basketball with her five brothers and sister. Her brothers would treat her as if she were one of them. Little did they know the rough-housing and stern treatment would help cultivate her endurance and strength. These 2 traits would forever be burned in her memory as a constant reminder that she is strong enough to conquer the world.

Other than the usual duties of cooking and cleaning, Ann had a talent of all talents. One that surpassed everyone in her family…her voice. She could sing you a happy song and add a little joy to your life. She started singing as a little girl with her family. They would sing around the house, outside in the community, and whenever they went to church. She loved to sing. She could brighten up even the most somber mood by singing just 1 note. Her melodic voice was known throughout the region, and people would travel for miles just to hear her sing a few songs. It gave her a sense of purpose. A feeling of self-worth with a touch of pride. This talent was all her own. Holding her head up high, an overwhelming sense of inner peace came over her every time she sang. An air of class with a graceful style unique only to her.

*

One evening, Albert decided to go on a date with a woman he met in town. He took her to a local juke joint establishment frequented by the locals on a Friday night. A juke joint was a place where African Americans would go after hours that featured music, gambling, drinking, and dancing. These places were primarily located in the southeast part of the United States. The word juke is derived from "juk", a Gullah word meaning disorderly or infamous. The buildings were generally small, with a few tables and chairs. A bar was off to the side where all kinds of drinks could be ordered. A stage was in the back with enough space to hold a piano, drums, and guitar. Sometimes, a trumpet or saxophone player would be there to add to the band. A microphone was set up in the middle for a soloist. Owned and operated by African Americans, juke joints provided an escape from the day-to-day struggles of life. For some, it was their only source of entertainment and recreation in life. An outlet to take their minds far away to a happy place of refuge.

Albert had gone out for a fun night and was enjoying himself. The mood was light, and everyone was laughing and talking, until a woman walked onto the stage. The lights dimmed, and all eyes turned to her as the spotlight came on. When Albert looked up, he saw a woman so beautiful it made him pause. Her smile was bright, and she seemed full of life. But when she opened her mouth, her voice was unlike anything he'd ever heard. It felt like she was singing just to him.

The room fell silent as Ann began to sing. She closed her eyes and bellowed sweet tones of alto while singing "That Reminds Me" by Della Reese. Her red dress was made of satin with hints of lace on the sleeves. Her black patent leather heels looked slightly worn but still had a bright, glossy shine. Her pearl necklace hung just below her neckline. Her silver bracelet sparkled on her wrist. The dark red lipstick she wore accentuated the fullness of her lips. As she sang, her hard life seemed so distant. She was in her element. Her comfort zone. Her happy place.

As soon as Albert saw Ann, something in his heart changed. He excused himself kindly from his date, knowing it wasn't polite, but he couldn't ignore what he felt. Normally, he'd never leave a woman alone, but this moment felt like fate. However, this woman on the stage was different. She was special. She was unique. While approaching Ann, his knees felt so weak that they might give out. He introduced himself and complimented her singing talent.

Ann thought, "Who is this man all dressed up?" She knew expensive things when she saw them. He had a stiff blue button-down shirt with a sharp collar. His black dress pants were starched with a crisp crease. His black leather lace-up dress shoes looked brand new from the shoemaker. A shiny silver watch with a large face was on his right wrist. On his right hand was a silver pinky ring so large that no one could miss it. To top it all off, he had a black sports jacket that added class and a look of debonair charm. Ann knew that he must be a hard-working man to have all these expensive things because the average black man couldn't afford what he had. She looked up, saw his warm smile, and smiled back at him. That's the moment Albert knew he had her.

There was one problem. Ann had a very stern father and 5 protective brothers. Albert wanted to take Ann for a date, but he had to cater to them first. So, he met with her father, who was very impressed but dared not to show it. In those days, the father of the home was treated with the utmost respect. He was to be feared among the children and respected among the adults in the community. And it didn't help that her father happened to be 6 feet 5 inches tall. He towered over everyone he encountered. His voice was very deep and raspy, when he spoke, the room seemed to vibrate from his low monotone. They had a conversation that consisted mainly of questions from her father. He asked questions such as where Albert was from, what he did for work, and who his people were. Albert was nervous but answered all the questions and made a great impression. Her father allowed Albert to take her on a date under one condition. All 5 of her brothers had to go on the date with them, and Albert had to pay the bill. This wasn't customary, however, it was the only way for him to go out with Ann. Albert agreed and took everyone to the picture show in town. They went to see the movie It Happened on 5th Avenue. It was a charming and uplifting movie that was popular at the time. He was so glad just being with Ann that he didn't mind taking her brothers at all.

*

Ann's father was so impressed that he granted Albert her hand in marriage. The family was thrilled because Albert had enough money to support Ann and the family fully. They were impressed with his work ethic and determination to have the best things in life. Her father had heard about Albert throughout the community and knew of the respect for him not only in the Black community but also in the White community. At a young age, Albert had already garnered a reputation for integrity that far exceeded all his peers.

Albert was just 19, but he had already spent years taking care of his family. He knew what it meant to support a woman and children and make sure they had what they needed. Since he was 12, his days had been focused on helping his mother, sisters, and brother while taking care of himself. Because of Albert, they lacked nothing. He knew that this next stage of his life would require even more hard work and dedication. He now had a family of his own. He loved challenges and was more than ready for this next chapter in his life.

The Big Move

As soon as they got married, Albert and Ann began growing their family. Albert kept working for Mr. Charlie, caring for the animals and driving the tractor. The fields had to be worked every few weeks. He liked harvest time best, knowing he could now bring fresh food back for his wife and kids, and also share some with his mother and the rest of his family. When he wasn't on the farm, he was working with Mr. Wilson on all types of jobs. It seemed everyone needed to have their sink unclogged or pipes replaced. Two days out of the week, Albert would work for Mr. Rainey. Customers had electrical problems, such as circuit breaker and wiring replacements. Albert could fix them all and was very reliable. The workdays with Mr. Jones were by far the longest and hardest of all the different specialties. These jobs were the new construction of buildings in town. A small grocery store, an insurance company, and a bank were just a few of the major projects. The workdays were especially hard because they were mainly done outside. Sometimes it was as hot as 95 degrees, and other days as cold as 34 degrees. Even though these jobs were the most strenuous, they made him more money than the others.

He could easily provide for Ann, but the way of life in the South seemed to be getting worse. Albert knew that to provide a safer environment for his family, they would need to move away. He didn't want to leave his mother and siblings, but he had a wife and children to care for and provide a better future. He wanted his children to have more opportunities than he had growing up. Looking back at his childhood, he knew he needed to move out of the state to provide those opportunities. One important opportunity he often thought about was a better education. His circumstances limited his education, and he didn't want his children to suffer a similar destiny.

So, after much thought and careful consideration, Albert decided it was time to move. But move where? He could get a job anywhere with his skill set, so work wasn't an issue. He decided to discuss this dilemma with Mr. Charlie, who treated him like a son. Mr. Charlie had family in New York and told Albert to inquire about some opportunities there. Albert took his brother along and traveled to upstate New York. He heard many different things about New York. Some good and some bad. He knew there were more opportunities to make a good living, but it was also faster paced. It was heavily populated even during that time and was one of the fastest-growing states in America. Nonetheless, he was willing to step out on faith and take a chance.

*

He had enough money to buy a house and looked for one first. He found one in no time. It was a decent-sized, single-family house with many steps to climb just to get to the front door. From the road, it had white siding with black shutters for the trim and a black shingled roof. As he approached the front door, he noticed a large porch with plenty of space for seating. The front door opened onto a hallway and more stairs on the right side. To the left was a living room. It wasn't a very big room, but enough for a couch, a recliner, a coffee table, and a television. It did have a rather large coat closet and 3 oversized windows. Albert liked natural light, so the windows were welcoming. The door on the opposite side of the room led to the dining room with another large window. Off the dining room was a tiny sitting area big enough to hold a small loveseat. As he walked through the dining room, he saw the kitchen. It wasn't too small and had all the necessary appliances. The white linoleum needed to be replaced, and the countertops seemed worn and old. The door to the basement was in the kitchen. The basement was unfinished and a great space for storage. He had quite a bit of tools and they could easily fit down there. Albert knew he could certainly fix everything he saw so far.

He walked back down the hallway and started up the stairs. At the top of the steps was the one and only full bathroom. It had a tub with a shower, a sink, a toilet, and some built-in shelving. As a child, he had to go out back to the outhouse in the fields to use the bathroom. So, this bathroom was a dream. Just past the bathroom was a hallway with the master bedroom on one side and another bedroom on the other side. The 4th door in the hallway opened to another set of steps. These steps led to the finished attic, which housed 2 additional bedrooms. Albert was impressed and went back downstairs.

He stepped into the backyard to have a look. It was small, but the kids would have just enough space to play. A run-down metal shed stood in the back corner. About fifty feet away, a wooded area stretched out with big rocks and tall trees. He knew he'd need a fence to keep the little ones safe. That was no big issue. He learned how to install different types of fences back at home. Wrought iron, chain link, and wood panel fences were some of the easiest. Other than that, the backyard would work just fine. With some minor improvements, this house was just right for Albert and his family.

The house was located on a quiet street at the top of a hill. The hill was steep due to the mountainous terrain of this small upstate New York town. The street was lined with single-family homes on both sides. It was very narrow, especially with cars parked alongside the sidewalk. None of the houses had driveways or garages, making it impossible to drive more than 5 miles per hour on the street. Most of the homes were multilevel homes with front and back porches. Trees and wooded areas encompassed the rear of each house. Looking down the street over the trees, each house had a view of the quaint downtown area. Just beyond the downtown scene was a picturesque view of the Hudson River. On a clear sunny day, the river glistened like fine crystal. The mountainous terrain bordering the river created a tranquil tone that seemed to soothe the soul. This town, located in Westchester County, was Peekskill.

*

Peekskill is a historic town alongside the Hudson River in New York State. Located about an hour north of New York City, it was founded in the late 1600s by Jan Peeck. She is the first known person to encounter the Lenape Native American tribe. They were native to the lower Hudson Valley area. The name Peekskill is derived from her last name and the Dutch word "kill", meaning stream. It was first settled in the 1700s and was characterized by its European style. It soon became an important Revolutionary War military base and housed army officers from 1776 to 1782. The landscape was a perfect defense location due to its hilly and wooded areas. George Washington established his headquarters at the Birdsall House in the town, which is now one of many historic sites in Peekskill. A few other historic sites include the Peekskill Freight Depot, where Abraham Lincoln gave a speech after being elected and the United States Post Office, which was built during the Great Depression as an economic stimulus.

Perhaps the most notable are historic sites linking Peekskill's ties to the Underground Railroad, a network of sites that helped enslaved people travel to freedom. The home of William Sands and the home of famous abolitionist Henry Ward were known as "Safe Houses". The Park Street A.M.E. Zion church was well known as a safe place also because its members included Harriett Tubman, Sojourner Truth, and Frederick Douglas. These sites helped between 60,000 and 100,000 slaves gain freedom between 1820 and 1861.

Peekskill was always known for its ingenuity. During the Revolutionary War, the mills made leather, planks, flour, and gunpowder. The area was also known as a major supplier of stoves, iron plows, and brick pavers. Peekskill Chemical Works is known for inventing Crayola Crayons, which are used all over the world. This small river town is full of rich history and unique charm, attracting people from all over the country.

*

After paying $8,000 for the house, Albert headed back to South Carolina to bring his family. The moving truck was loaded, and they all said their farewells. The trip to New York felt long and tiring. There were only a few highways available for travel. They often went through small towns and big cities, making long-distance travel very time-consuming. But after several stops and 15 hours later, the family of 5 made it to their destination, a new home in the state of New York.

Now, Albert needed work to continue to support the family. He started by doing handyman work locally in the community. Word spread that a jack-of-all-trades from out of town lived in the area, and soon his side jobs became his main source of income. But he still needed a job with benefits for his wife and children. One morning, while fixing someone's roof, he overheard talk about a General Motors plant in a nearby town. He got excited about the idea of applying, but he knew he needed a high school diploma. One of his daughters stepped in right away and helped him study for his GED. Then he was ready to apply. His interview went so well that they hired him right away. Even though he had no formal training in electrical, plumbing, and construction, the management considered his wealth of experience and hired him for maintenance.

He went home to tell his family, and Ann celebrated by baking one of her famous pound cakes. The children at the time were overjoyed because this meant nicer things. They would often talk about their dream clothes, shoes, and stuffed animals. Their favorite doll at the time was Chatty Baby. The girls really wanted her and knew Albert's new job would bring them closer to having her. Barbie dolls also became popular, and they were able to have Barbie dolls too. Everyone in the family was elated about this new job and all the blessings it brought.

GM

William C. Durant started General Motors in September 1908 as a holding company for Buick in Flint, Michigan. In 1916, it became a public company under the name General Motors Corporation. It soon acquired Chevrolet, GMC, and Cadillac car makers. General Motors now operates manufacturing plants in 35 different countries around the world. Headquartered in Detroit, Michigan, it was the largest and fastest-growing automaker in the United States. It carried such a wide selection of cars and trucks that anyone in the market for a vehicle could find a car that fit their budget and style. Albert was familiar with GM and looked forward to working for a company with such a high reputation.

While working at General Motors, Albert exemplified hard work. After getting hired, he focused on using all the knowledge that he had gained over the years. The strong foundation from his youth gave him an edge that most maintenance workers didn't possess. His duties at work included fixing heavy machinery, maintaining the facility, and breaking down equipment that was no longer needed. Management was so impressed by Albert's ability to troubleshoot and fully fix the machines that they offered him a supervisor position. He politely declined, stating he could make the most impact as a maintenance worker and trainer. He wanted the new maintenance workers to be fully efficient after training. The only way to ensure that was to train them himself. His passion for fixing things and handling issues when no one else was around demonstrated his integrity. His positive attitude, even from childhood, pushed him to try and fix everything. In his mind, no problem was too hard to fix. He made sure to stress that to all his coworkers.

The work environment soon became a place of fulfillment. His coworkers enjoyed the feeling of working on a team. Teamwork helped ease everyone's job, decreasing employees' stress, which allowed each worker to concentrate on the details of every product being made. They developed pride in their work because the quality of the work was at an all-time high. Every morning, the employees looked forward to getting to work. Each evening, they would eagerly share with their families all the wonderful products they made, projects they were working on, and the overall satisfaction they felt from working at GM.

*

Soon, Albert gained several friends while working at the plant. These men admired Albert not only for his hard work on the job but also because he was a family man who took pride in providing for his family. He never missed a day of work. Even when he wasn't feeling well or his body was tired, he would still press on to work. Other maintenance men took notice and began to mimic Albert's persistence. Everyone looked forward to lunch breaks with Albert. They crowded around him, asking questions about his younger years and where he came from. They wanted to know how he became such a team player and how he pushed others to be their best.

A friendship was formed between the maintenance men and Albert. A friendship that would last for the next 35 years and extend far beyond the bright white walls of the automaker.

When the crew was off work, they would keep in contact with one another by telephone and, when possible, would sometimes meet outside of work. The plant would close for all Federal holidays. Some of the maintenance workers took turns hosting different holidays. Memorial Day was Albert's. He'd throw a cookout and invite his coworkers and their families. The backyard always had plenty of chairs, and several brown wooden picnic tables were set up along the right side. A row of lawn chairs lined the back edge of the yard. The grill was located on the left-hand side of the yard. There were several chairs around the grill for guests who liked to watch. Dark green shrubbery bordered the yard, sprinkled with bright white and pink flowers throughout. Since Albert loved all his family, he would invite extended family members and friends who lived in the area. The sound of music could be heard all the way down to the bottom of the street. An old radio station played popular songs everyone knew. Various artists of the time, such as Ray Charles, The Drifters, The Supremes, and Sam Cooke, were quite popular. Everyone would sing along, and a few family members would get up and dance. Laughter filled the air as a few friends even tried to sing along.

    Everyone would bring a dish to share. The food was always delicious. Hamburgers were thick and juicy on sesame seed buns. The hot dogs were slightly charred with a smoky flavor. Some of the guests brought fruit salads filled with grapes, strawberries, cantaloupe, and watermelon. Others brought creamy coleslaw and baked beans full of onions and spices. Ann made the best potato salad. All the women wanted her recipe, but she only shared her secret recipe with her daughters. Along with Lays potato chips and drinks such as

Pepsi, Kool-Aid, and water, these cookouts were everyone's favorite place to spend Memorial Day.

Albert was a mentor to those men, always encouraging them to do their best. Always looking out for the others, offering support and motivation. One of the men he helped was John, the youngest technician and the newest to join the General Motors team. Albert wanted to see him succeed, so he shared everything he had learned over the years. He taught John how to adjust the machines properly and how to keep them running smoothly week after week. When one of the assembly lines went down, a series of troubleshooting steps had to be followed. Albert was so knowledgeable that he could pinpoint the failure just by simply looking at the machine. John followed every procedure Albert showed him and paid very close attention to each step given.

During a training session, John forgot to shut the clamp on one of the extruder machines. As they moved away, Albert heard a faint clicking sound coming from it. No one else seemed to notice it. However, Albert knew these assembly lines like he knew how to ride a bike. So, he could tell when something wasn't quite right. He started inspecting the machine and found the problem immediately. John apologized, and Albert told him that everything was alright, and everyone made mistakes. "The key is to learn from them," Albert explained. Albert shared this and other lessons with everyone he encountered. No matter what the mistake, Albert would lift them up and encourage them.

John learned so much from Albert. As a young man starting a career, John knew that hands-on learning was important, but learning from a seasoned person was even better. He applied the tips Albert shared with him from his personal work experiences to his work.

*

Retirement was bittersweet. Albert was a pillar at General Motors while working there for 35 years. He would brighten up one's day with a kind word and encouragement. So many lives were impacted by his willingness to not only do his job but also help everyone around him do their job. The quality of work that came out of this factory was superior and exceeded any other car manufacturing plant in the region.

Even after he retired, people still talked about Albert and the years he gave to the job. He left his mark on every assembly line in the plant. Some of the ideas he came up with solved mechanical problems for good. He created solutions that weren't temporary but a permanent fix. His critical thinking skills were valued at the highest levels because his solutions saved the company thousands of dollars every year. All the maintenance workers had Albert's phone number and would call him for advice if they couldn't fix a machine. The workers were so grateful for his expertise and willingness to keep in contact and help them excel at work. In turn, they checked on him and his family regularly. For instance, some of the maintenance workers would visit the family at Christmas. They brought their families over along with gifts and food. Some of the gifts were colorful crochet blankets, dish sets, glassware, and other household items that the entire family could use. Foods such as cookies, fruit baskets, pound cakes, apple pies, and other holiday treats were also dropped off. Everyone loved to visit this home during the holidays.

Albert left an impression on General Motors and its employees that is remembered to this day. His positive attitude and thirst for improvement left a legacy of growth and persistence. Because of him, they were able to find joy and a sense of purpose in their work.

Largest Family in the Block

Back at home, the family grew to 10 members. Ann was busy taking care of all 8 daughters. She also cleaned houses for a living. She would travel to the next town to perform cleaning duties such as dusting and mopping. She washed, folded, and put the clothes away. She would strip the beds and remake them with fresh linens. Even the tablecloths would be washed and ironed perfectly, along with the cloth napkins that laid across each charger on the dining room table. Most of the houses had carpets, and vacuuming daily was a necessity. Ann knew how to vacuum in such a way that symmetrical lines were present in the carpet of each room. As she went from room to room, she made sure to rid the windows and mirrors of any smudge marks. The baseboards throughout each house were wiped off regularly, giving the look of a squeaky-clean home. She had a key to each house and would let herself in and out after several hours. The homeowners trusted her, and she was loved by entire families for her attention to detail, so much so that they would give her rare paintings for her own home.

Meanwhile, Albert was busy working at General Motors. Life was a challenge. Juggling each family member's schedule was rather difficult. Each daughter had a talent and various extracurricular activities. There were voice lessons and piano lessons, to name a few. Ann grew up singing. As a child, she sang at home and in church. Her love for singing was passed down to her daughters, who also loved to sing. So, to accompany their singing, some took piano lessons. Lessons are usually twice a week. The piano teacher lived 2 blocks away, and the girls would walk together, hand in hand. Others took voice lessons, which were also twice a week. The voice lessons were around the corner in a little white house. Each lesson lasted an hour, and the girls would skip home in time for dinner. Ann and Albert believed in helping all their daughters develop their individual gifts and committed time and money to them.

*

Ann always rose early on Sundays to make her homemade biscuits. She'd mix flour, baking soda, sugar, and salt in a large bowl. Then came the butter, followed by a splash of milk. She stirred it all together with a wooden spatula until it formed a soft dough. She spread flour on a board and folded the dough several times on top of the flour. She used her hands to flatten the dough. She didn't use a rolling pin because her mother always told her she could feel when the dough was ready if she used her hands. Using a biscuit cutter, she made close cuts straight down into the dough and transferred each biscuit to a baking sheet. Baked for 12 minutes at 425°F, the biscuits rose to perfection. The family woke up to the aroma of buttery goodness throughout the home.

After the biscuits, Ann would first get all 8 daughters ready for the day by pressing their hair. She had an ironclad comb called a hot comb. She placed it on the eye of the stove until it got extremely hot. She would part their hair and rub hair grease such as NuNile on each patch of hair. She would comb through the hair, making it shiny and straight. This was a task that took some time because she wanted all her daughter's hair to look the same. Next, Ann ironed their frilly dresses one by one. Some wore cream-colored dresses and others wore gray. Each dress would hang just below their knees. Each daughter also had black patent leather dress shoes. Ann would shine the younger daughters' shoes, and the older girls would shine their own. They would all run downstairs for biscuits when they were dressed and ready to go.

This was a musically gifted family. Ann and Albert sang every chance they got during church services. Most of the songs were hymns and old Negro Spirituals, with the spirituals being their favorite. Two of their daughters were talented piano players, while the others sang alongside their mother. The church members always looked forward to hearing the whole family sing. It was always a treat for the entire congregation when the family would come together and sing as a group. Standing side by side, each daughter would sing until the heavens heard and rejoiced. Tones of alto and soprano were heard along with a strong tenor from Albert. He learned at an early age from his mother that singing soothed the soul. He instilled this in all his daughters and shared it with his church and community.

The church itself was a pillar in the community. Mount Olivet Baptist Church began as a small prayer meeting in the late 1800s. In 1901, it was officially named the Baptist Church of Peekskill. Then in 1910, a new building was erected, and Mount Olivet Baptist Church was formed. The building was a beautiful light brown brick edifice. It had a grand set of stairs leading up to the front door. After walking through the vestibule area, 2 double doors opened to a beautiful sanctuary. The flooring was wall-to-wall, lush red carpet. The wooden pews lined both sides of the aisle leading to the front. At the front, 2 choir stands were on either side of the pulpit. The musician's area was to the right, complete with an organ and drum set. Many powerful sermons were preached there, and people would travel from all over the area to hear a good Word and fellowship with the community.

After church, they would hurry home for Sunday dinner. Sundays were the only days the family would have meat with dinner. During the week, butter beans and biscuits provided a filling and tasty meal every night. A large pot of butter beans and biscuits was the cheapest meal, and yet could easily feed a large family. Ann would slow-cook the cream-colored butter beans until they were tender and melted in your mouth. They were lightly seasoned with salt, onions, and cracked black pepper. But on Sundays, chicken was a delicacy. It was golden brown and fried to crispy perfection. Ann learned how to cook from her mother, and family recipes had been passed down for decades. Fried chicken Sundays were a treat the entire family looked forward to.

Back during that time, dishes cooked for special occasions and holidays included macaroni and cheese, collard greens, potato salad, and candied yams. Desserts almost always included a pound cake and sweet potato pie. These recipes were timeless, and each family member had their own version. Some would add double the brown sugar to the yams. Others would use different cheeses in their mac and cheese instead of just cheddar. Yet some would even use turkey legs instead of ham hocks in the collard greens. Either way, the food provided comfort and nostalgia for the young and the old.

*

Albert had the largest family on the street. All the neighbors knew him. One day, he was walking up the street and noticed a man trying to fix his gutters. Albert offered his help and fixed the gutters in no time at all. He would help anyone, anytime, anywhere, with anything. Soon, word spread about Albert's expertise in home improvements. He would get calls from all the neighbors needing things fixed, from leaky roofs to plumbing to faulty wiring and circuit breaker boxes.

He could fix it all, and he proved it time and time again. There was no need for a plumber or an electrician in town because Albert was called for everything. And he didn't mind at all. In fact, he loved his community and would do anything to build it up. As a child, he witnessed neighbors and friends sharing resources such as food and clothing with his family. In return, his mother would mend torn clothes and make new clothing, such as sweaters and dresses, for their neighbors. It was a continuous cycle of helping one another not only to survive but to thrive. So, Albert saw the results of helping others throughout his life. Every community he was a member of improved and flourished. Because of his handyman skills, all the houses on his street and the surrounding areas looked well-kept. There was no chipped paint, torn siding, broken windows, or patchy roofs. Even the yards were trimmed and neat with brightly colored flowers. The community felt like home.

One day, Albert was called to fix some steps at Roy's house down the street. As he approached the house, he noticed several small children playing in the front yard. There was a metal washboard on the side of the house, and clothes drying on a clothesline. While fixing the steps, he decided to get to know Roy since they were neighbors. Roy explained that he lost his job and is looking for work. He also said their washing machine stopped working, and they are washing all their clothes by hand. After Albert fixed the steps, he asked to look at the washing machine. Roy said yes and led him down the narrow hallway to the washer. He started explaining to Albert that he didn't have the money to fix it. Albert looked over it anyway and took it apart. He found the problem. An attachment holding the drum in place had popped. This was normal wear and tear and happens all the time. Of course, Albert knew how to repair it. Since the family needed help, Albert made a trip to the nearby home improvement store to get the supplies for the washing machine repair. When he got back to Roy's house with the items, Roy's wife was waiting on the porch, her eyes filled with tears. She couldn't believe someone was selflessly helping them. Albert got to work, and in no time, the washing machine was quietly running again. Albert always believed that he should go out of his way to help others, even if that meant spending his own money. He knew that whatever he did to help someone in need would come back to him and his family in the form of blessings.

When Albert got home that evening, he shared what he saw and did with Ann. He told her that Roy had lost his job, and the family was struggling to make ends meet. Ann wanted to help, too. She decided to share some of their beans since she had so many bags. She sent the oldest daughter down to Roy's house with 5 bags of dried butter beans. Albert wanted to do more, and invited Roy to apply to General Motors. He told Roy all about GM and his work duties there. Roy stated some of his own work history. He worked for several auto repair shops as a mechanic, completing tasks such as oil changes, brake replacements, and tire rotations. He also helped with engine repairs, such as gasket and belt replacements. Radiators and water heaters were a speciality for Roy because he had at least one per week to work on. Albert assured him that his past skill set should help him get the job. Two weeks later, Roy received the phone call he was desperately waiting for. He was now an employee at GM.

Another neighbor, Ms. Booker, lived 2 streets over and had 4 children. Her husband passed away several years ago, and she was barely getting by. She couldn't afford to fix anything at her house. All she could do was provide necessities for herself and the children. When Ann bumped into Ms. Booker at the grocery store, she could see that something was wrong. They chatted awhile, and Ms. Booker confided that her house was falling apart, and she couldn't afford to fix it. Ann went home and talked to Albert about the situation. Albert always had extra supplies at home. He and Ann walked down to visit Ms. Booker one Saturday afternoon. They toured the house to get a better idea of what needed repair. The list wasn't too long, and Albert was eager to get started.

First, the gutters were hanging down off the house onto the ground. He fixed the gutters by nailing them back up and cleaning them out. Next, he went inside the house to replace some of the kitchen floor tiles. They were peeling and sticking up from old water damage. He replaced them with bright white tiles. While in the kitchen, he also unclogged the sink that wouldn't drain properly. Throughout the house, the carpet was worn and ripped. Albert replaced all the carpet in the house. Also, he fixed some of her furniture that was broken. The legs on the chairs and tables were loose, and he tightened them. Her dresser was leaning due to a broken leg, and he fixed that. Some of her doors were hanging by the hinges, and he tightened all of them. When he completed his to-do list, he told Ms. Booker to call him or Ann if she needed anything fixed in the future.

Albert strongly believed in serving his community. He felt that by making the community better, he was helping to create a safer, stronger place for his children and others to grow. This mattered deeply to him because he had faced many struggles during his own childhood. He couldn't be a child or do childish things. He was thrust into adulthood at an early age and didn't want that to happen to other children. He made up his mind to do his part and make life better for all.

To Future Generations

The legacy Albert left for future generations is one of strength and purpose, rivaling that of some of the world's most admired men. People who knew him caught only a glimpse of the hardships he endured. From the moment he was born, he carried a determination that guided him through life. His faith was the glue that held him together and provided a rock to lean on in times of trouble.

He lived by certain principles that he alone was accountable for. One principle was simply to work hard. He believed that hard work always paid off in the end. He stood on the Bible verse Colossians 3:23. It says," whatever you do, work at it with all your heart, as working for the Lord, not for human masters." From a young age, Albert understood that working hard and doing his best helped improve his life. He found real satisfaction in finishing a job, no matter how big or small. Whether he was solving a problem at work or handling something simple at home, he always felt proud when the work was done. He would always stand back and gaze at his work with a smile, proud yet humbled by all the opportunities he was given throughout his life.

Working hard also gave his family a way out of poverty. As a child, he witnessed some of the lowest points life has to offer. His childhood home was nothing more than wooden boards. He had to choose work over education as a 12-year-old boy. And he had to learn new things, such as heavy machine operation, in a short time. Eager to propel forward into a better living situation for himself and his family, he worked as hard as he could. Because of his dedication to all that he did, his example will continue to live on through his children, grandchildren, and beyond.

Another principle he lived by was never to pass over an opportunity for growth. He leaned on the Bible verse Phillipians 4:13, "I can do all things through Him who strengthens me." When presented with an opportunity to learn a new trade, Albert never declined. His willingness to explore new occupations opened doors for him that no other man with a 7th-grade education could accomplish. His skill set qualified him to be able to build a house all by himself. Years of experience in plumbing and electrical issues provided very specific specialties that weren't easy to come by. Few plumbers and electricians existed in the small river town where he lived. Also, his experience in construction opened another door of opportunity. He was able to build a frame, put up drywall, pour concrete, lay a roof, install siding, and much more. This knowledge not only proved lucrative but also helped him repair his own home and that of his family.

"Therefore, whatever you want men to do to you, do also to them..." is the Bible verse from Matthew 7:12. This verse pushed Albert even further toward his life goals. He watched as his mother, Mr. Charlie, and countless others gave selflessly of their time and resources to anyone in need. This is also portrayed in the Leviticus 19:18, which says "...Love thy neighbor as thyself..." Albert helped his neighbors and the entire community with all sorts of home repairs. He would lend a helping hand with church projects as well. He added a second sanctuary to the church. Larger community projects, such as restoring historic buildings in town, took longer to accomplish. Albert would lend his expertise wherever he was most useful.

Yet another Bible verse and personal favorite was Galatians 6:7. This included "…whatever one sows, that will he also reap." His mother would tell him about this verse, and it resonated throughout his life. Albert sowed a seed of never giving up and focusing on the future. He shared this with all he encountered. They saw his willingness to keep pushing and learning, no matter how long it took. His siblings and everyone in his family saw how hard he persevered and the vast rewards he reaped afterwards. They followed his footsteps as they got older and taught their children as well.

Also, he seemed to have everything he needed. This came from sowing seeds of generosity. Albert didn't just help people; he went above and beyond by attempting to supply as many of their needs as he could. Some neighbors needed costly repairs done to their homes. Others had food insecurities and needed help feeding their families. Then there were those in the community who just needed someone to talk to. Albert was generous with his money as well as his time. In return, he always had money in his pocket. He was given numerous opportunities to earn money through various jobs that paid very well. He was always paid in cash and had money all the time. It was a continuous cash flow of giving and receiving. Sowing and reaping. Even at 12 years old, he would have enough money to do whatever he wanted. This was because of all the different jobs he was trained in. He was always paid in cash and had money all the time. His family members learned from his example and followed it.

Grace was another seed sown in his life. As a young boy, he only remembers seeing his father once. Growing up without a father made life challenging, especially during the 1930s. Abandonment, despair, and anxiety were just a few of the feelings he had to overcome. Challenging as they were, he always reverted to grace. His mother often spoke of Hebrews 4:16. She reminded him that as we approach God's throne of grace, we may receive grace to help in our time of need. He reminisced about his father with grace. This led him to forgiveness. This also taught his siblings, wife, and children that grace is necessary in living a full, joyous life. In turn, his interactions with others showing him grace allowed him to accomplish great things. He was afforded better opportunities, allowing him to take care of himself, his family, and all who were connected to him.

One day, he and his mother were working outside in her garden. They were harvesting some of the vegetables and got to the row of mustard greens. These greens had full green leaves. A few long stems were in the middle with tiny yellow flowers on the top. These long stems had small green pods hanging from them. Susie took one of the pods off the stem and opened it up. They were the tiniest black seeds Albert had ever seen. She placed a few in the center of his hands. About the size of a pen tip, they rolled around easily, almost slipping through his fingers. She told him they were mustard seeds. Matthew 17:20 says that if you have faith the size of a mustard seed, you can move mountains. His mother wanted him to understand that anything is possible with even the smallest of faith. Just a hint of faith could allow him to accomplish any goal he set for himself.

One of Albert's main goals was to take care of his family. He was willing to do whatever it took to make sure they had what they needed. At times, the challenges in front of him felt hard to face. He knew moving to New York was the right choice, but the thought of starting over with no job was always in the back of his mind. Leaning on his faith, he made the decision and didn't turn back. He believed that everything would be alright if he just stepped out on faith and trusted in God. He was right! The house, the job, and all that followed were a direct result of his faith, which only made his faith stronger for the rest of his life.

Another goal he had since adolescence was to have a successful career. Dropping out of school at such an early age dimmed his hopes as he grew older. A 7th-grade education can severely handicap anyone trying to obtain a good job. A job with benefits worthy of retiring from. He had strong faith, though. Determined to succeed, he used his years of experience in different fields to apply for a job that he seemingly wasn't qualified for. This strong showing of faith landed him one of the best jobs he ever had, with a title and career he could be proud of.

At the time, having any job at GM was considered somewhat prestigious. GM paid more than any other company in the Hudson Valley region. The benefits, which included insurance such as medical and life, were outstanding. Perks such as paid holidays and bonuses helped raise the status of most families from poverty to upper-middle class. It was apparent throughout the community who worked for GM and who didn't. Those families had larger homes on average, with 3 or more bedrooms and could accommodate even a family with 7 or 8 children. Every employee could afford a decent car. Albert had a large station wagon which had enough room for the whole family. This elevated lifestyle was made possible through his successful career as a maintenance technician. A career that he and his family were proud of.

Albert made a lasting impact on his family, his community, and even the world around him. He lived by biblical principles and practiced them daily to help make things better for the generations that followed. The example he left behind was shaped by his culture, his personal reflection, and a deep drive to be his best. Though he started with very little, he built a full and meaningful life, one with all he needed and even some of what he wanted. The example he set for his family, the community, and the world was one that all should follow. He lived a life that will live on forever through all he touched.

Words To Live By

Faith

- Hebrew 11:1 " Now faith is the substance of things hoped for, the evidence of things not seen."

- Hebrews 11:6 "It's impossible to please God without faith because the one who draws near to God must believe that He exists and that He rewards people who try to find Him."

- Proverbs 3: 5-6 " Trust in the Lord with all your heart, and do not lean on your own understanding. In all your ways acknowledge Him, and He will make your path straight."

- Matthew 21:22 "And whatever you ask in prayer, you will receive, if you have faith."

- Matthew 17: 20 "Truly, I tell you, if you have faith as small as a mustard seed, you can say to this mountain, 'Move from here to there,' and it will go. There will be nothing that you can't do."

- Mark 9:23 "Jesus said to him, 'If you can do anything? All things are possible for the one who has faith."

- Mark 11:24 "Therefore I say to you, whatever you pray and ask for, believe that you will receive it, and it will be so for you."

- John 3:16 "God so loved the world that He gave His only Son, so that everyone who believes in Him won't perish but will have eternal life."

- 1 Corinthians 16:13 "Stay awake, stand firm in your faith, be brave, be strong."

- 2 Corinthians 2:5 "I did this so that your faith might not depend on the wisdom of people but on the power of God."

- 2 Corinthians 5:7 "For we walk by faith, not by sight."

- Romans 10:17" So faith comes from hearing, and hearing through the word of Christ."

- 2 Timothy 4:7 "I have fought the good fight, finished the race, and kept the faith."

- Ephesians 6:16 "Above all, carry the shield of faith so that you can extinguish the flaming arrows of the evil one."

- James 1:3 "After all, you know that the testing of your faith produces endurance."

- James 1:6 "Whoever asks shouldn't hesitate. They should ask in faith, without doubting. Whoever doubts is like the surf of the sea, tossed and turned by the wind."

- James 2:24 "So you see that a person is shown to be righteous through faithful actions and not through faith alone."

Humility

- 1 Peter 5:6 Therefore humble yourselves under the mighty hand of God, that He may exalt you in due time."

- James 4:6 "But He gives more grace. Therefore, He says, 'God resists the proud, but gives grace to the humble."

- Philippians 2:3 "Do nothing from selfish ambition or conceit, but in humility count others more significant than yourselves."

- 2 Chronicles 7:14 if my people who are called by My name will humble themselves, and pray and seek My face, and turn from their wicked ways, then I will hear from heaven, and will forgive their sin, and heal their land."

- Ephesians 4:2 "Be completely humble and gentle; be patient, bearing with one another in love."

- Proverbs 11:2 "When pride comes, then comes shame; but with the humble is wisdom."

- Proverbs 22:4 "By humility and the fear of the Lord are riches and honor and life."

- James 3:13 "Who is wise and understanding among you? Let them show it by their good life, by deeds done in the humility that comes from wisdom."

Determination

- Philippians 4:13 "I can do all things though Christ who strengthens me."

- Jeremiah 29:11 "For I know the plans I have for you, declares the Lord, plans for welfare and not for evil, to give you a future and a hope."

- 2 Thessalonians 3:13 "As for you, brothers, do not grow weary in doing good."

- Proverbs 16:3 "Commit your work to the Lord, and your plans will be established.

- Psalms 27:14 "Wait on the Lord; be of good courage, and He shall strengthen thine heart: wait, I say, on the Lord."

- Luke 1:37 "For nothing will be impossible with God."

- Galatians 6:9 "Let us not become weary in doing good, for at the proper time we will reap a harvest if we do not give up."

- James 1:12 "Blessed is the man who remains steadfast under trial, for when he has stood the test, he will receive the crown of life that the Lord has promised to those who love Him."

- Psalms 37: 23-24 "The Lord makes firm the steps of the one who delights in Him; though he may stumble, he will not fall, for the Lord upholds him with His hand."

- 2 Corinthians 4: 8-9 "We are hard pressed on every side, but not crushed; perplexed, but not in despair; persecuted, but not abandoned; struck down, but not destroyed."

- Isaiah 40:31 "But they that wait upon the Lord shall renew their strength; they shall mount up with wings as eagles; they shall run, and not be weary; and they shall walk, and not faint."

Albert Morrison

From humility to greatness

Humble to exceptional

Invisible to significant

This comparison can go on forever

A lowly life from the start

An ascending rise to the unknown

Many have come before

Many will come in the future

An endless road

Paved for the next generation.

About the Author

Kelley Ann Smith is a woman of faith. As a loving mother of 4, her faith in God has stood the test of time, the only constant in her life. As a teenager, she began playing the organ in church, a skill instilled in her as a small child by her father. His love for music, along with her mother's love for singing and praying, helped lay the foundation of her faith and love. It wasn't until later in life, after hitting rock bottom, that God picked her up and showed her the value of peace. The peace that surpasses all understanding. Her quest for true peace through the Word of God set her life on a new and exciting path, a new season in her life filled with abundance and a hope that she spreads to all she touches.

References

Britannica.com

History Channel/history.com

Archive.tuskegee.edu

www2.oberlin.edu

detroithistorical.org

The MacArthur NKJV Study Bible

Bible App Share You Version

www.ingramcontent.com/pod-product-compliance
Lightning Source LLC
Chambersburg PA
CBHW061235070526
44584CB00030B/4129